rima fragmenta

Fifty Sonnets for Kevin

rima fragmenta

or

Fragments of a Rift:
Fifty Sonnets for Kevin

AC Benus

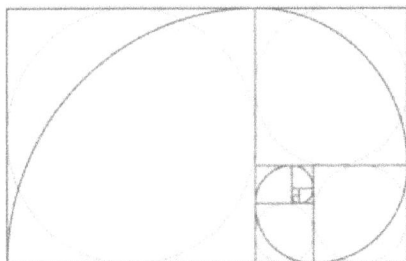

an AC Benus Impression
San Francisco

Grateful acknowledgement is here offered
for the support and encouragement
I've received on the literary site
www.gayauthors.org.

I would specifically like to mention
the following authors for their assistance with this project:
Lyssa; Mikiesboy; mollyhousemouse;
Parker Owens

THANK YOU!

ISBN 978-1-7345610-0-5 (ebook)
ISBN 978-1-7345610-1-2 (paperback)

RIMA FRAGMENTA, OR FRAGMENTS OF A RIFT:
FIFTY SONNETS FOR KEVIN.

Cover photo:
www.pxfuel.com

Golden Ratio vignette:
www.freepik.com

Library of Congress Control Number: 2020901453

"... del vario stile in ch'io piange e ragiono
fra le vane speranze e 'l van dolore,
ova sia chi per prova intenda amore,
spero trovar pietà, nonché perdono..."

Francesco Petrarca

Sonnet No. 1

Like a boy with his finger in the dyke,
For too long I have been staunching the flow;
Yet, to let loose brings hope and fear alike
That emotions may overwhelm me so.
But from the blockage of my heart I must
Slowly withdraw the thumb of obstruction,
Letting deluge be the thing I entrust
Buoys my words atop deep seduction.
Now, in this quiet moment, comes your thought
To lift these relocations in your hands,
Above tensions with my worries held taut,
And ensure this love Time itself withstands.
    Drown I just might, but I want to believe
    A flood of you will allow me to breathe.

Sonnet No. 2

Your kisses have the substance of sunlight –
Your breath across the surface of my lips
All the murmurs of creation ignite,
Casting murky fear in paltry eclipse.
As if it were but yesterday, I see
You sitting on the bed, your nervous smile,
Head dips and narrowed eyes across from me
In the half-light to utterly beguile.
Just before we touch that very first time,
You moisten your mouth as you close your eyes,
Letting Space draw shut on our paradigm
And excite a new existence of sighs.
    Yet, of all the times we kissed, the first just
    Confirmed we are nothing if not stardust.

Sonnet No. 3

In the stillness of your room, I can turn
To catch your reflection – which is perfect –
Hover behind me in lingering sojourn,
As we join deeper than the intellect.
Reality is but a division,
A refracting of both present and past,
Like a mirror standing in apprehension
To observe wistfully, yet be steadfast.
Your breath hastens; your stroke glides down my back;
Thus the true-life looking glass on the wall
Lets me admire you, and all your knack,
Fill the sheath between us without withdrawal.
   Awestruck observer and participant,
   Every part of you now leaves an imprint.

Sonnet No. 4

Never have I so much felt like Alice,
Stretched through the glass, or lost in Wonderland,
As your arms slid 'round me without remiss
And pulled me to you so I'd understand.
After our first lovemaking, hands entwine,
Heads lay on pillows and eyes inspected
The depths of souls to there try and divine
The other felt what we both suspected.
No 'Drink Me' potion, no Mad Hatter tea
Ever invited like your looks did then,
So I let me fall in your gravity,
Feeling every closed part of me open.
    Not through a rabbit hole, but soaring high,
    You draw like the pull of a starry sky.

Sonnet No. 5

Chronos himself has sought an age to learn
    secrets borne by the Butterfly Effect
    with its conundrum mighty and direct,
do small nudges stable states overturn?
Here, chicken-and-egg questions we discern,
    wondering of love if desires project,
    or passion rules of attraction affect,
for since your first kiss, I the answers yearn.
    Your brightness with the room is contrasting,
    lifting my legs to hover face to face,
    about to feed me and end my fasting
    with the bareness of you and your grace –
    set to penetrate memory everlasting
    when sex and love were born in one embrace.

Sonnet No. 6

When personalities get in the way;
When age seems to be a factor; when race
Plays a part – where these command undue sway –
Links don't form, but with us it's not the case.
Such thoughts are absent when I'm in your arms,
Like on the day my hands could first explore
How firm your muscles and soft your skin charms
The coaxing caress you seem to adore.
Oh, Kevin – not age nor station matter
To the quality of our sweet union,
For when our differences are together
The new light we make is bright communion.
    In contrast is balance too; such a truth
    Outweighs our looks or age, our race or youth.

Sonnet No. 7

Icarus had wings made by his father,
The power of which to him were unknown,
Yet he spread them without too much bother,
Knowing the life he risked was but his own.
Lying next to you reminds me of how
Our spirits may be borrowed devices,
Granted in freedom, but which can allow
Soaring vantage over grounding crisis.
So, like the boy from his prison-escape,
I unfold my gift when I am with you,
And though I glide near the warmth of your shape,
I don't fear you melting me through and through.
  For when our souls find room to stretch and fly,
  Even stars must melt in a lover's sigh.

Sonnet No. 8

In Love's embrace, time's measured in heartbeats –
A dance like Figaro's *tune* called by Fate,
Or the *Grecian Urn's* perfection by Keats –
The eternal in the now incarnate.
So, what of us will be worthy to last
Through the years of uncertainty and change,
If not a chance to connect with the past
As a living spark where love's the exchange.
How others will judge and view my feelings
Is a power that their brains will decide –
But it's from the heart I seek the stealings
Which let us live again and Death deride.
    When joined, it's we who name the final song,
    The one where life is short but art is long.

Sonnet No. 9

We have to rouse because your sister's dog
Waits patiently for us in the front room,
But to delay our parting epilogue,
I'll walk her with you and our chat resume.
Every aspect I see sparkles; your mind,
Through kindness and intellect, reaches out,
And with your interest in me intertwined,
Reflects back as a smile most devout.
Chore complete, and back into the half-light,
Our goodbye of hands on waists, and locked gazes
Will hardly find release in what I write,
For everything you do amazes.
    Like when you say you want to see me once more,
    I can part from you still richer than before.

Sonnet No. 10

If I pause and wonder at it, I see
Perhaps you have no notion just how bad
Your sudden cutting off contact hurt me,
Muddling the joy of your memory with sad.
How hard is it to construct a past tense? –
An 'it's over,' with certain surety –
But with no goodbyes, you left me in suspense,
Doubting even recall's security.
No questions rise on how you made me feel,
Knowing for certain your thought will not fade,
When to words I have recourse that can deal
A blow to doubt and all the sorrow it's made.
   A lover's complaint, but why did you go –
   Did I deserve to be treated just so?

Sonnet No. 11

Your email's full of anticipation
Keen as a kid awaiting Christmas morn;
Only, the pleasures we'll unwrap are homespun,
With clothes alone in danger of getting torn.
I greet you at the door and thus begin
The longstanding way we will reunite:
Hands and eyes locked, hearts pumping adrenaline,
Lips coming together as we both lose sight.
Nothing ever seems so right as your kiss;
No embrace ever returns such longing,
For equanimity is its own bliss
When both feel the decisive belonging.
    Like a child knowing Santa must be real,
    Belief itself proves the greatest appeal.

Sonnet No. 12

On the street, lost in the whirl of the world,
I oft times become drawn by the currents
To let my vision settle where allowed –
On someone still amongst the human torrents.
That one – say, a handsome young man – on his own,
Attracts my empathy like a magnet,
For though he and I are seemingly alone,
Separate isolation may find joint outlet.
How different to sit by myself in a room
And contemplate our tender intersection,
For you and I never have to assume
Distance equals a lack of connection.
    In thought alone or lost in fleshly riot,
    Being with you is contemplative quiet.

Sonnet No. 13

The poet lovers once explored a land
Where Mother Nature's bounty overflowed;
Where milk and honey on the desert sand
Gave promises only Time could erode.
And so, seeing your smile when I dipped
The perfect strawberry in the syrup
Recalled in me the sensual manuscript
Where the ink of body and mind line up.
The morsel brought to your lips for a bite
Smothers the sweetness of a New World
Where Rimbaud's rose the deepest kisses invite,
And Verlaine's passions to the depths are hurled.
    Explorer, or the land that is conquered,
    We long most for the place our hearts are spurred.

Sonnet No. 14

"And all the pleasures we shall prove" still yields
A landscape of delight for our demesne,
But "hills and valleys" are not the far fields
Rhetoric strikes, but my lips staking a claim.
They glide in confident survey, noting
Every divot my Sir finds most intense,
And in your lordly enjoyment gloating
How my skill beats your sensual defense.
For words are words, and flesh is flesh for aye –
As long as comforts move them together,
Equals they meet and never have to say
"Live with me and be my love" forever.
    Yet, if that holy word should slip from me,
    Let it roam free where it can simply be.

Sonnet No. 15

Whether trained on stars, or locked on the ground,
   you spin me like the hands of a dervish –
   one up to capture, one down to impoverish –
surging through the vessel *me* to redound.
And in that tumult, your kisses abound,
   caressing my neck, finding the ear which
   channels your passion to heavenly pitch
as your weight on me feels deeply profound.
   And then, a pause; a crying out erupts –
   a new rhythm for us is suddenly born
   in pulsations to fill me body and soul.
   No pleasure is ever new or abrupt
   that rushes from the moment life was sworn
   to let heaven and earth in us lose control.

Sonnet No. 16

Our minds alter all they will encounter –
Its touch Midas-like makes matter golden;
Its scorn debases like any doubter –
And to its judgments we seem beholden.
Yet freedom and soaring heights are there too,
Like Sappho's far-branched apple just in reach,
But hidden from the pickers in plain view
Because they never the obvious beseech.
And so my love for you I change each time
I think of your smile, unguarded and free,
Gilding rays of sunshine with thoughts and rhyme
While reaching for what's plainly before me.
    Memory is both a blessing and curse;
    Our wings to heaven and our earthly hearse.

Sonnet No. 17

Why is it every time I close my eyes,
The sweetness of you comes within my sight? –
Why when I stop my ears from my own sighs,
Your dulcet timbre vibrates in delight?
Oh, Kevin – these hands ache for your embrace:
These arms and feet pressed against your chest,
Lips parted, quenched, but striving for your face,
Waiting for the moment of union blessed.
    Gradually, your efforts slow and then cease –
    But I feel you, your weight pressed against it;
    That quivering pause before a great release –
    And in me, I absorb every last bit
    Till your form descends upon me in peace
    To make your memory in me permanent.

Sonnet No. 18

In my vision, the pentecostal flame
May descend in hues of red vermilion,
But burning is not its most ardent aim,
Converting believer from civilian.
Your hands are just the same, burnishing me
Like an agate iron, to liquefy
The thinnest gold sheet that my skin may be;
To not destroy, but enlight my mind's eye.
So when your forceful grip commands my flesh,
It's as convert I willingly submit,
And know my precious soul is thus refreshed
Once your tool glows hot from my passions lit.
    A new faith, a new creed is in your caress;
    An evangelical end to my distress.

Sonnet No. 19

Curtains rustling, libations newly poured,
We rest on the daybed outside, *fresco*,
Pausing our pleasure before its encored
With *shisha* vapor, laughs and *prosecco*.
Though so much of life is filled with upset
Roiling beneath everyday commonplace,
In hedonistic calm are worlds beget
Where past and future bow to present grace.
So, beautiful's the look cast when you raise
The mouthpiece to your lips and tease out smoke;
Perched on your cushions in mystical ways,
Carroll's shrew caterpillar you invoke.
    Hookah and toadstool, it's our hearts we prop
    With moments as fine as a champagne drop.

Sonnet No. 20

Each time I sit down to pick up a pen,
Like fog the moments of sadness appear
To confuse the happy memories when
Connection was all we had to hold dear.
The choice is mine, and I know it quite well,
To allow present misuse to obscure
The gone-beauty of what I've yet to tell,
And make of my glory something demure.
So, vaporous clouds of doubt, I ask you
To not bring reality raining down,
But let my internal light now shine new
And dry tears of a smile turned from a frown.
    Is it fair to always ask the same thing...
    How much peace can "you hurt me" really bring?

Sonnet No. 21

Scattered sunlight forces through the teak blinds,
Animating your moves almost like film,
While your freshness seems like all of mankind's
Before our clay was fired in God's kiln.
My hands, at home enlaced about your neck,
With summer air stirring all around us,
Invites newness as we laze upon my deck;
My seat in your lap encountering no fuss.
Somewhat blinkered, I feel your forceful grip
Baking you in the wet-earth of my soul
With incessant rhythms that well equip
The passionate light you ever control.
    Leading man experience, or real life,
    I'm your starlet to de-script every strife.

Sonnet No. 22

The cliché would say he sleeps like a rock,
But the truth is – he sleeps like an angel –
For when he released me from his lovelock,
He dozed and left me to be chronicle.
In dreams we often view reality
Through the mirrors of a better perfection,
Which when awake will seek finality,
Despite the quirks of our own reflection.
Yet, like a Shakespearean character
Worked in poured-alabaster flawlessness,
He's touched by no one but his protector,
Given His divine and human caress.
    To watch over him as he sleeps and nods
    Grants artistic license to rival God's.

Sonnet No. 23

If with us there is a re-set button,
One in touch with the cosmos to undo,
Would I wish to retract and keep it in? –
Un-say my words that I'm feeling for you.
Bravely at the door, our second goodbye,
I let slip this sex has got to mean more,
For how we connect will harbor no lie,
Sheltering us in half-truths to ignore.
But the way you react tells me I error,
That no part of you wants to now admit
Kinship with the piece of me just laid bared.
You kiss, look concerned, and make your exit.
    So, words are words – even those left unsaid –
    No un-told lie's ever better instead.

Sonnet No. 24

Once I watched you depart, I wondered if
You'd see me again; if the door I closed
In aftermath of my verbal mischief
Pronounced a sentence most gravely imposed.
Why do we fear to come into contact
With thoughts welling emotions from inside? –
Is it instinct causing us to react,
Or merely self-preservational pride?
But then I recall how your kiss lingers,
Feel how easy doubt is to demolish
Thinking of your hand grasping my fingers,
To assure me my contact's not selfish.
    If you hold on, then let me be your guide;
    We'll crack your heart, and do it side by side.

Sonnet No. 25

Our third appointment, I but open the door,
   And you instantly bend me to your kiss,
   Making my mind draw near a precipice,
Which your hands insist in maddening encore.
Cradled in the crook of your arm, I adore
   How your touch explores every orifice
   You intend to transform *sui generis*,
And make love to me like the stuff of folklore.
   In absolutely blissful mandatory
   Swooning under your possessive manly power,
   It's hard for me to say when I've ever known
   Love beyond this yet greatest allegory –
   Compelled to surrender 'neath a kissing shower –
   Like a falling star having the heavens shown.

Sonnet No. 26

Cardplayers and songwriters know even
There's sometimes nothing to replace the blues;
By the way I feel, that maxim's proven
When chords in my head play win, draw or lose.
So when you contact me, I should exalt
To know my sin of truthfulness – my fault –
Is expunged as long as I don't assault
The silent treaty where my words I halt.
Thus like a song on eternal repeat,
Hands of Aces build to larger pattern
But follow the metre of a heartbeat
Unsure what to do, or which way to turn.
　　But my whole gamble is its sum gestalt –
　　Holding song and cards from you by default.

Sonnet No. 27

Imperfections make us approachable –
Our shortcomings allow us connection –
And faults broken down are manageable
When judged 'gainst unimpeachable action.
From amongst the many things I can do,
Making you love me is not one of them.
So, with flaws, if I were a bit more true,
Would you surrender to my stratagem?
Yet, how vulnerable can people be
When they hide nothing from sight? –
My unapproachable strength may not free,
But being yours body and soul just might.
    All I know is what I feel in your arms;
    If unspoken, it's still love there that charms.

Sonnet No. 28

Could my impact be but a passing blow,
Lightly minted on your temporal flesh,
Like a bruise to heal and quietly go
Beneath a bandage's all-soothing mesh?
And yet, I think of a rock hurled in space
Whose topsy-turvy tumble will not end
Till encount'ring a larger body's face,
Where through fire, their outer shells transcend.
So don't think I've only touched you lightly,
For when our bodies became one, there was
Light between us to outdo the nightly
Sky with its painted twinkles all abuzz.
    I know you're deeply altered by my touch;
    The way you hold back says to me as much.

Sonnet No. 29

Hedonistic – the word makes you catch your breath,
Smile and bite your lower lip just the way
You do before you die that little death,
Peering through my eyes, seeming my soul to weigh.
How often life will make of us the figure
Sung in the spiritual known as *the motherless child*,
But what pain or sting of gladness can trigger
These feelings of longing and love unreconciled?
So in the *petite mort* I see in your eyes
A certain form of comfort settles in,
Like a parting of the clouds in the skies,
Scatt'ring my fears of soulless oblivion.
    I'm found when lost in your body's advance,
    For your raptured hold's like a great expanse.

Sonnet No. 30

Once you had ceased talking to me, how sad
Each and every creativity seemed
To my dark-painted projections unclad
From your beautiful wont; undreamed.
Goethe said mastery of form only shows
When limitation of order is gained,
For then an ultimate freedom bestows
Discipline to the youth age has obtained.
Now the back of the hand writing looks old
Where a collection of wrinkles gather
As if my father's fingers I behold
Taking here my cast than his own rather.
    But I'd trade all my agèd accomplishments
    To share a few artless more of your moments.

Sonnet No. 31

When viewed from the vantage of the cosmos,
We live but a fleeting day, like a spark
Cast from a campfire to drift morose,
Until alone, we finally fade to dark.
Tempus fugit – often how have we heard;
Carpe diem – no time like the present;
Such concepts used to seem far from the Word
And clichés to ignore as unpleasant.
But every Truth remains to find the way,
Among the drifting embers of our mind,
To reignite what's real and have us say
"Though life is short, it's love I seek to find."
    So, from the distant, stellar point of view
    Our chance to connect flies before we're through.

Sonnet No. 32

In life, few times are our expectations
Bettered or best by a reality
Knocking the wildest imaginations
Down with flesh-and-blood sensuality.
And so we are blessed it looks when your hand
Decides to enfold mine within a cloud
As soft as a billow, but firm as land,
Laying my dreams abed in your arms' shroud.
Too many are the sensations you give
When your love surmounts Reason's shortcomings;
Too many are the daydreams that won't live
'Cause the realness of you serves them drubbings.
   'Fantasy,' I hear you tell me with spite;
   If so, why then hold me with all your might?

Sonnet No. 33

The golden means seeks to find a middle path
Between extremes where the twain will not meet;
The golden ratio unfolds beauty's math,
Be it in leaf, flower or a star's heat.
So when I'm with you, my spiral expands
To limits without outer boundaries
Where the core of me can shake off demands
Presented by the world's confounderies.
But along the middle way, exploring
All the wonders you trace out before me,
Our ratio I will keep balancing
To unlock the swirling stars' finite key.
    Eyes opened or closed, it does not matter;
    The light of you great patterns still scatter.

Sonnet No. 34

The Bard wrote of having the love of his boy –
Professed his ability to absolve
Every perceived wrong with a grinning ploy –
Yet here I sit with nothing but my resolve.
Perhaps not ready to confess it yet,
Your acts speaker louder than any poet
When our ebb and flow produces the sweat
Any man would envy as proof of it.
So, can great love be a one-sided conceit;
Move in but one direction as it were;
Act in the manner of a one-way street?
No. For true give and take can be singular
    No more than a river can run opposed
    Within its banks as two currents enclosed.

Sonnet No. 35

Perhaps a quota each lifetime consigns
   Which suggests what we get as a leeway
   When avoiding the rules we must obey
As love comes around, and our heart entwines.
So, can a life unfold in fourteen lines? –
   Reduced in manner to struggle and say
   I'm more than my sum of parts can convey,
As long as my soul with hope realigns.
   I do not know, is the simple answer,
   And yet I look to you to understand
   All the meaning my words try to confer,
   Regardless where on the spectrum they land,
   For a love that's great never should defer
   To questions of where those two people stand.

Sonnet No. 36

From thence, our lovemaking forms an archetype;
Where at least once a month we reconvene;
Bliss clouds around us as if from a pipe,
Causing happiness to take on our sheen.
In the heat of our summer, my fingers
Trace the satin sweat cooled along your spine;
Your "Sorry" like a smiling boy's lingers,
But I tell you "No, I love that it's mine."
Thus, a new order is established too
As "I love it" falls gently into place;
Summer heat's a substitute to renew
The 'I love you's allowed no breathing space.
    Ergo, when you fall on me, and I feel
    The moisture on your skin, I know what's real.

Sonnet No. 37

For the viewer, beauty has the feel of
All the connections of eternity,
For it is through this processing of love
The timeless achieves non-duality.
So, when we turn and lie still and silent
With our touch being the only focus,
Limits melt away and our fears relent
Almost to the point beyond our notice.
There in the heart of quiet acceptance
Do we become mortality's equal,
Gazing at beauty's undying expanse
Lacking no beginning, end or sequel.
    What matter words when everything else speaks;
    When your palm decides to cradle my cheek.

Sonnet No. 38

Sometimes I sit and marvel at your strength –
At times, I should say, barely able to sit –
For your excitement with me knows no length,
While your cache of reserves appears infinite.
In throes, I'm like Lawrence's character,
Counting stars on the back of closed eyelids,
Where each image of you melds to a blur
Of celestial forces and wingèd cupids.
Your power gifted is unstoppable –
Springing free from the eternal store of God –
I feel both mystic and desirable
As my darkness in your light is over-awed.
    Like Lady Chatterley, I must admire
    The endless stars you seed to inspire.

Sonnet No. 39

In his stately pleasure dome, Coleridge said,
Kublai Khan lacked for nothing – even boys –
To distract the keen omnipresent dread
That everything he must love, he destroys.
So in our drifting puffs, a cloud is there
To obscure the ground upon which we walk,
Grasping with blind hands for what we most care,
When all the words have turned to merely talk.
But, my mind, the big tent of our pleasure,
Floats above intermittent THC
To elevate our seeking together
For the deathless bonds of fraternity.
    Like a poet's high, all I need's belief
    For cares and concerns to poof in relief.

Sonnet No. 40

It's hard to tell if anything was good
When viewed through the curtain of my tears,
Wondering if this therapy ever could
Negate the hurt of these past several years.
Do you think I could forget that last glimpse
Of you come back to my door to accuse? –
No, for to do so would make us both wimps,
And in the balance, it's Love who would lose.
So, even though your eyes were brimmed with scorn,
I'll now remember it by forgetting
How you left me cold that bright sunny morn
To contemplate my penance of accepting.
   For ridicule deserves none of the same
   If it reduces feelings to a game.

Sonnet No. 41

The master phrased it best, that the North Star
Is ever-fixed while armillary rings
Protract points of light to horizons far,
Etching harmony amidst the superstrings.
My love is like Polaris, unbending;
Though the position of your heart has changed,
Mine's steadfast with no mind of pretending
What we two most enjoy's not preordained.
So let others 'round this love revolve
To admire the night sky's beauty here,
For even heavenly bodies evolve
Once a more-perfect model is made clear.
    Although the celestial circus is slow,
    Rapid burns the fires for all who know.

Sonnet No. 42

Of the many comforts we enjoy, the times
We've snuggled to rest beneath the moonlight
Now prod my napping talent for the rhymes
Worthy of the sweetness of our "good night."
Yet, the crush of my inadequacies
Upon all such surges of the life force –
Which others tap with nar' a hint of unease –
Drive my efforts to dream a hopeless recourse.
How I'd like to sketch out here the ideal
Of your muscled strength in my grasping hold,
While we mount the higher passions which reveal…
But alas, perhaps my soul is not so bold.
    These attempts spur me on and on to sing,
    Abed in both the joy and pain they bring.

Sonnet No. 43

The way your lips trace the curve of my neck,
Following the line from lobe to shoulder;
Your kingly breath trailing in its slow trek
To cool and fan flames up from a smolder;
All these sensations you give, and then more
While we cuddle in dawning's fresh air
Devouter than the priests by ancient score,
For your arms are answer to every prayer.
There is no turning point when we're like this,
No nagging doubts or fears I must banish;
No past, present or future in this bliss,
Just a space where intangibles vanish.
    So please never let your hold on me release;
    Keep me sovereign and prelate without cease.

Sonnet No. 44

Getting up, I've steak and eggs to arrange,
But you grin like the Sphinx to slow me down,
While our two positions you interchange
And press behind my knees, making no sound.
How can I not at such a moment say
I love you, Kevin, with all my being
Letting your counterbalance hearts to weigh
Anubis-like with your eye all-seeing.
So, measure me out while I'm in your grip
And discover no faithlessness in me;
Instead, sink to our core relationship
And come to the point you set both souls free.
    Light as a feather, you know we fly as one,
    Leaving flesh behind to join our father, Sun.

Sonnet No. 45

Seven are the holy numbers which spin
    Across our spine and emotions imbue
    Kaleidoscopic points of every hue
When we activate the Chakras within.
To do so, we merely need imagine
    Our higher and lower selves rendezvous
    On an internal plane where bonds subdue
The fears weakening loving discipline.
        For when you reach my inner midst, there's peace –
           As if rainbow shards of color alight
           And display the balance universal
           Obtained the moment of Creation's height
           When gyroscopic wheels became sacral –
        You spin me root to crown without release.

Sonnet No. 46

We can never say goodbye properly;
What starts off as a handshake in the hall,
Turns hugs, kisses – bags dropped entirely –
Then held hands and movements back to the brawl.
At these times, there's never past or present;
Satiation or starvation of souls;
Only connection endlessly content
To don and slough mortal/immortal roles.
Downstairs we seek out and find anywhere
Serving convenient for our urgent need:
Staircase; rug; doggie bed; library chair;
Each has been blessed when our love has been freed.
     Hunger's neither a blessing nor a curse
     But a way to unseal the universe.

Sonnet No. 47

Draftsmen will say you must have drawn five miles
Before claiming much mastery of the line,
But what then of poets, we metrophiles,
Drawing on clouds and rainbows for design?
How many words must we write to persuade
An order and control onto our heart,
Expounding the soul not to act afraid
All while we bleed ink and tears for our art.
Answers are not here, or at least for each
The number of lines the mind must draft –
Or the treaded miles of patience they teach –
Varies by a single degree of craft:
    For expression is not about any form;
    Without love, it's but a practice to perform.

Sonnet No. 48

Love is a gift we give ourselves, it's said,
But what other munificence offers
Self-charity to live beyond the dead
With nothing but words stuffed in its coffers.
You may not find here those earthly riches
Only to be sought on the temporal plane,
And think my love merely moans and bitches,
Loudly mourning your absence and disdain.
But to a higher purpose we're both led
When mind to mind there's no question within
That what's ordained in benefice is fed
All the treasures of the world that's ever been.
    Doubt me if you must, if it feels better,
    But accept this our deaths can unfetter.

Sonnet No. 49

There through a hushed moment, I watch you snooze
Beneath slanting sunshine amongst the hours
My fingers have chance to rove, wondering who's
Luckier than we in this love of ours.
Your thought still spins me around – makes me smile –
Though the sweetness of the present's gone,
I've encircled the past for just a while,
Like a captured rock in your orbit drawn.
But when my caress strokes your arm just so,
Your eyes open to mine and those lips part;
Your hand draws me like it'll never let go,
To kiss me like Time itself we'll outsmart.
    This feeling is something to hold onto
    As memory delays the final adieu.

Sonnet No. 50

I know this book's no work of art, at least,
It's far from what I'd nursed in my vision
Of a tale to tell of spirit not decreased
By the loving intent of its decision.
In the end, you'll think my work is a stunt,
Planned and executed in dull hubris,
Because my love is something you do not want
And use that knowledge as a thing to dismiss.
But for this poet, there's no pretending
What passed between us left no impression,
For like a pentecostal flame unending
You're burned in me like a deathless expression.
    But now, I'll let tears flow and put this to an end;
    Just know, I wish you the best, my beautiful friend.

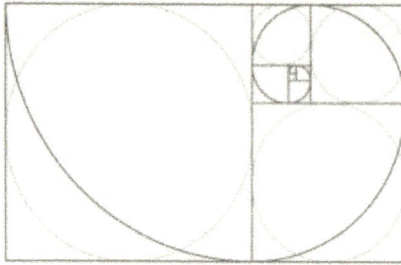

www.ingramcontent.com/pod-product-compliance
Lightning Source LLC
Chambersburg PA
CBHW021919040426
42448CB00007B/826